The Kids' Guide to

Digital Photography

How to Shoot, Save, Play With & Print Your Digital Photos

Jenni Bidner

SCHOLASTIC INC.

New York   Toronto   London   Auckland   Sydney
Mexico City   New Delhi   Hong Kong   Buenos Aires

EDITOR
Joe Rhatigan

SENIOR ART DIRECTOR
Chris Bryant

DESIGNER
Jenni Bidner

PHOTOGRAPHER
Jenni Bidner

COVER DESIGNER
Barbara Zaretsky

ASSOCIATE EDITOR
Rain Newcomb

EDITORIAL ASSISTANCE
Delores Gosnell

PRODUCTION ASSISTANCE
Shannon Yokeley

PROJECT DESIGNERS

Pamela Smart: Pages 58 and 61

Suzanne Tourtillott: Pages 59 and 60

SPECIAL PHOTOGRAPHY CREDITS

Steve Mann: Pages 58 through 61

© Meleda Wegner: Author photo

© Eric Bean: Page 3

Sandra Stambaugh: Pages 8, 26 (top), 28, 29 (top), 45 (bottom right), 46 (top)

John Widman: Page 46 (bottom right)

Wolf on pages 10 and 11 photographed at the Wildlife Science Center, **www.wildlifesciencecenter.org**

ISBN-13: 978-0-439-93382-7
ISBN-10: 0-439-93382-X

12 11 10 9 8 7 6 5 4 3 2   8 9 10 11 12/0

Printed in the U.S.A.   40

First Scholastic printing, February 2007

Contents

Introduction

DIGITAL PHOTOGRAPHY IS A LOT EASIER THAN YOU THINK!

It's easier than photography with film, because you know instantly whether you got the shot or not. And it's a ton more fun because you can share your cool results with friends just seconds after you take a picture.

But what about the computer side? Well, if you can play games on your computer, then you have just about all the skills you need to get started with a digital camera. All you're really doing is taking a picture with a mini-computer (your camera) and transferring it to your desktop or laptop computer. Once on your computer, you can save it, copy it, or transform it into a new artistic creation.

Best yet, you can shoot, and shoot, and shoot, and shoot—and never have to spend a dime on film and processing. Paper and ink cost money, but when your allowance runs out, you can always share your pictures through emails (free!) and maybe even your own website.

So, what exactly does digital photography involve? Well, that's what this book is all about. But for a jump-start, you can turn to the Ten Steps to Success on pages 7 and 8 to see how easy "going digital" really is. Then try some of the neat techniques for taking great pictures. You can even turn your awesome pictures into cool crafts, gifts, and other fun stuff. But most of all, go out and enjoy your camera.

With this book, you'll be able to...

- Figure out everything you need to get started taking digital pictures

- Find out what kind of digital camera is best for you

- Use terms like "jpeg" and "megapixel" with a confidence that will make your parents jealous

- Save your pictures so that they're the right size for emailing, printing, and putting on your website

- Turn your scanner into a camera

- Find out how all those little buttons on your camera work

- Take great pictures of friends, pets, vacation spots, sports action, and even yourself

- Borrow techniques from the pros to make your pictures even better

- Manipulate your photos on your computer to make them look better or just plain wacky

- Create cool things, such as stationery, pet portraits, and more using your digital photographs

1

Digital Basics

Most digital cameras are so easy to use, you can just pick them up and start shooting good pictures. But a few digital topics, such as resolution, are important to understand if you want really good shots.

What's a Digital Picture?

A digital picture is simply a photo that has been converted into "computer language" and saved as a file. A digital camera takes pictures without film. You can also use a scanner to convert prints and film into digital pictures.

Once on your computer, you can open the picture file and the computer displays the picture. Just like most other computer files, a digital picture file can be saved on your hard drive, as well as on a recordable CD. It can be attached to an email and sent over the Internet, or posted to your website.

You can alter or play with your digital photos, and then print them onto special paper so they look just like the prints you'd get from a photo lab. And finally, you can use specialty papers to turn your pictures into great crafts and projects (see chapter 4).

Ten Steps to Success

Digital photography can sound scary, but it's not. It's really just plain old regular photography, except instead of film, the camera takes the picture on computer memory. Here's the whole process from start to finish in 10 easy steps:

1 LOAD MEMORY INTO YOUR CAMERA

Load the camera with a memory card or memory stick. This is the digital equivalent of film. (A few older or cheap digital cameras don't have removable memory.)

2 ERASE OLD MEMORY

Format the memory card or stick so there are no pictures on it. But wait! If there are pictures that you want to keep, you'll need to transfer them to the computer first (see step 6) or you'll lose them forever!

3 SET RESOLUTION (PICTURE SIZE)

Select the resolution or picture size you want. In average situations, with a camera that shoots low resolution email-sized files, you can hold over 160 on a 16 MB card or over 600 on a 64 MB card.

High resolution pictures on a three or four megapixel camera will eat up memory a lot faster, creating files that are 2 MB or more apiece, meaning 32 or fewer pictures on a 64 MB card (see pages 9 to 11 for more details).

4 SHOOT GREAT PICTURES!

It works just like a film camera. See chapter 3 for shooting tips.

5 TRANSFER TO COMPUTER

Download the images to your computer. This can be done by connecting the camera to the computer (with a cord or wireless), or by removing the memory card or stick and putting it in a reader. It's usually pretty easy to do, but read your instruction manual if you have trouble.

6 SAVE THE PICTURES

Transfer or save these pictures into a folder. Use the default folder (such as "my pictures") or create your own special folder.

7 OPEN & EDIT PICTURES

Open the pictures on your computer with photo-editing software. Delete the bad pictures. Keep the good ones.

8 ERASE OR CLEAR MEMORY

Once you're sure the good pictures have been transferred to the computer, erase the memory card or stick. This command is called erase, format, or reformat. It can be done with the computer or with the camera.

9 BACKUP (COPY) PICTURES

Since there are no negatives, the file on the computer is now the only record of the picture. You may accidentally delete the image, or it could be erased if the computer crashes. Therefore it is a good idea to backup the best images, by making a copy on a CD, Zip disk, or other removable media.

10 GO OUT AND SHOOT SOME MORE PICTURES!

Don't worry if you don't know how to do all these steps. I'll take you through them in the rest of the book!

A Big Jigsaw Puzzle

A digital picture is like a big, finished jigsaw puzzle. But instead of puzzle pieces, it's made up of PIXELS. Each PIXEL holds a little piece of the picture on it, just like a jigsaw piece. When they're all lined up and in the right place, you can suddenly see the whole picture!

The more pieces (PIXELS) you have, the bigger the jigsaw picture can be. A camera that can shoot one MEGAPIXEL, means the picture has 1,000,000 *(one million!)* pieces. And five megapixels means five million pixels.

The number of pixels in a picture is also called its RESOLUTION. High-resolution images have more pixels, while low-resolution have fewer. Because a high-resolution picture has more pixels (more puzzle pieces), it takes more memory to save it in the camera and on the computer. In other words, it has a bigger FILE SIZE.

Resolutions

Most digital cameras give you a choice of what RESOLUTION (picture size or pixel size) to set before shooting your pictures. *So what's better? High or low resolution?*

Well, bigger is usually better, because a high resolution (two, three, four and five megapixels) picture means it will look really great when you blow it up into a big print. And while a low-resolution picture has a small file size (so it emails quickly), you can't print it big and hope to get nice quality.

It's sometimes hard to predict if that silly snapshot might become your all-time favorite photo, so when in doubt, play it safe and shoot at the highest or second highest resolution.

THE BIG BUT

Unfortunately, there are a few disadvantages to high resolution pictures. It takes longer for your camera to process the picture, which can lead to delays before the camera is "ready" to take the next picture.

The file size of a high-resolution photograph is much bigger than a low resolution picture. This means it will take more space in your computer's hard drive (it will take up more memory). It will also take longer to OPEN and SAVE in photo-editing or other software.

Worst yet, if you try to email a high-resolution picture, it could seem to take forever for the recipient to receive it, and it may appear huge on their monitor, requiring them to SCROLL to see the full picture.

resolution just right

resolution is too low

Resolution Solution

HIGH RES = BEST QUALITY + BIG PRINTS

LOW RES = FAST EMAILS + LOTS MORE PICTURES

How Big Is the Big Bad Wolf?

You're at the zoo taking pictures for the field-trip report. What resolution should you set?

If your camera only has one resolution setting, your choice is easy. But most digital cameras have two, three, or even more choices.

Now it's a tough call! If you go with the highest resolution, you may only be able to shoot a few pictures before all the memory in your camera is filled. But those pictures will be great quality, and you can blow them up to make HUGE posters. Or you can crop out a lot of the background and still have enough pixels for a good print. (See pages 52 and 53 for more information on cropping.)

On the other hand, if you shoot low resolution, you can take dozens and dozens of pic-tures without running out of memory. The more you shoot, the better chance you have of getting that one-in-a-million shot that will have all your friends going "oooh" and "ahhhh." But since they're low resolution, they won't print as well. They'll probably look great as email attachments or on the school website, but when printed in your report or for a wall display, the quality will go way down.

Before you make a decision, count up how many different kinds of shots you need for the project. Be generous in your count. This is the absolute minimum number of shots you need to come home with. Then add a few to the account for pictures of friends and fun stuff.

Just like a film camera counts down how many shots you have before you get to the end of the roll, a digital camera gives you a number as well. Check the information panel on the top of the camera when you have it set at a low resolution (small picture size), and you'll see a much higher number of shots than when you set it to a higher resolution (bigger picture size).

At the highest resolution are there at least as many frames as you need? If so, start shooting, and then use the MONITOR and PLAYBACK to edit as you go, so you can DELETE the bad pictures.

If not, reduce the resolution setting until the number of frames listed on the information panel matches the minimum number of photos you need.

Resolution Math!

As I mentioned before, the actual size of a digital image is usually stated in pixels, and the total number of pixels is its resolution. Resolution can be stated as a single number, such as 1,000,000 (one million or one MEGAPIXEL).

Resolution can also be stated as a math expression, such as 300x450 pixels (pronounced 300 "by" 450 pixels). This means the picture is 300 pixels wide, by 450 pixels long.

Surprise! Math quiz! The total number of pixels would be 300 times 450, or 135,000 pixels, because:

$$300 \times 450 = 135,000$$

Instead of having to write out a lot of zeroes, digital camera makers decided on the term megapixel to mean one million (1,000,000) pixels. Therefore a one megapixel camera can shoot pictures that are about 800x1200 resolution, because:

$$800 \times 1200 = 960,000$$

It's not uncommon to see five MEGAPIXELS (with a whopping 5,000,000 pixels) in a point-and-shoot camera.

JPEG File Formats

Most cameras shoot pictures in the JPEG file format, though some offer additional choices such as TIFF and RAW. Once in the computer any of these formats can be resaved into different file formats.

A JPEG file has a file name that ends with ".jpg" (note in some Mac and Windows programs, these letters may be invisible). JPEG is a good format for photos because it can show millions of colors, and therefore looks realistic.

It's also popular because it's a COMPRESSION file format that can be reduced to one-tenth the normal file size with little loss of detail. Compressed files take up less memory so you can shoot more before you need to DOWNLOAD (transfer) them to your computer.

MORE ON COMPRESSION

Compression comes with a price. As you make the file size smaller (COMPRESS the image), you will start to see a loss of detail and the picture will start to look bad.

The good news is that you generally can't see the difference until you start getting quite small (HIGH COMPRESSION). Medium to high quality (LOW to MEDIUM COMPRESSION) is okay for most photos.

Some cameras offer different compression options when shooting pictures. For the best results, select low compression (bigger file size and fewer shots per memory card or memory stick). In the computer, the COMPRESSION can also be increased to make a file smaller for emailing.

The COMPRESSION option usually appears in a PREVIEW window when you use the SAVE or

SAVE AS function in photo-editing software. Make sure the PREVIEW box is clicked, so you can watch the quality change. Continue compressing the image until you see a change in quality, then go up one or two levels in quality.

Other File Formats

If you receive email pictures or download images from a website, they may be GIF or BMP (bitmap) formats. These are two older file formats. Their only big advantage is their extremely small file size. The pictures don't always look good, because they are made up of too few colors.

Because website owners want you to be able to view their sites quickly, this smaller size is an advantage (GIF and BMP pictures

take very little time to download). Therefore you'll often see them on the Internet.

The TIFF format is a high-quality format, primarily used for professional printing and photographic applications and retouching. Some high-end cameras will shoot TIFF images. The files it creates are huge, because there is no COMPRESSION. For most home purposes, JPEG is a better choice.

If you're having trouble sharing pictures with your friends, RESAVE the photo as a JPEG. Usually this in done inside a PHOTO-EDITING software program, by going to the FILE command and then RESAVE command. Be sure you've named this new picture, so you don't ERASE the old higher resolution file.

HOW MANY MEGAPIXELS SHOULD MY CAMERA BE?

A megapixel equals one million (1,000,000) pixels. It sounds like a lot, but a one-megapixel camera is actually considered low-resolution camera these days!

■ **UNDER 1 MEGAPIXEL:** This camera is good for emailing and website fun, but not much more. It can't take a high enough resolution for good large prints.

■ **1 TO 2 MEGAPIXEL:** You can email and print regular prints on a home printer.

■ **3 MEGAPIXELS:** You can do all of the above, plus produce nice photo-quality prints (from home or a lab) up to 8x10-inch, 11x14-inch, or even larger.

■ **4+ MEGAPIXELS:** Even after cropping the image you can make large beautiful prints.

Choosing a Camera

Whether you're about to buy a camera, you have a great new one, or you're "stuck" using the family camera, you'll need to know what your camera can do. Not all the features mentioned in chapter 2 are available on simpler cameras, and the big, bulky professional-style cameras have a lot of complicated controls.

There are numerous types of digital cameras, ranging from ultra-simple low resolution models, to professional cameras costing thousands of dollars. The most common is the point-and-shoot style, but you can also get SLR cameras, or personal entertainment devices that merge pictures with MP3 music or cell phones.

Is Begging for a Digital Camera Not Working?

IMPRESS YOUR PARENTS WITH YOUR MATH SKILLS!

Do the math: Figure out the cost of one film roll plus processing, then multiply by the number of rolls the family shoots in a year. Your parents may be surprised how quickly you can "pay off" your new camera in savings. Of course, you'll need to consider the cost of inkjet paper and supplies for prints, but you'll find you don't print every image—just the very best.

POINT-AND-SHOOT

Point-and-shoot digital cameras are exactly what they sound like. You point, you shoot, and you usually get pretty good pictures.

Some point-and-shoot cameras offer many advanced features like specialized EXPOSURE MODES, while others are no-frills. They range from low resolution units suitable for emailing pictures, to megapixel models offering resolutions over five million pixels (see pages 8 to 11).

Point-and-shoot cameras are designed to be easy to use. Some really are, while others may seem very confusing with a dizzying number of controls. If you're skilled with a film camera, you should have no trouble with any digital camera.

DIGITAL SLR CAMERAS

Unless one of your parents is a photo-geek, you probably won't have a digital SLR (single-lens reflex) camera. They are big and bulky, and most have fancy lenses that can be removed and changed. *But wow!* Can they take some amazing pictures if you take the time to learn how to use them. Unfortunately, they're also pretty expensive, so if you wreck it, we could be talking about allowance or babysitting money for the next 10 years!

PICTURE-PHONES & MORE

Some cell phones, MP3 players, and other personal entertainment devices have built-in cameras or camera attachments. While these are great fun, the pictures are usually very low resolution. If your unit enables you to transfer the pictures to your computer, most will only be high enough resolution for emailing or small prints on your inkjet print-er. Few of them offer any of the advanced shooting capabilities described in chapter 2.

Many digital camcorders (DV) can also take "still" digital pictures. Most only offer low resolution—again good for emailing and small pictures, but not for big projects.

Point-and-Shoot

Cool Camera Features

If you've been shopping for digital cameras, you've certainly noticed that there are a lot of features to consider. The next four pages detail some of the most important features. Chapter 2 discusses in detail how to use many of them. And the chart on pages 18 and 19 can help you quickly decide which you really want or need.

Point-and-Shoot with Zoom

CONNECTION TYPE

The first step is to check compatibility. Can your camera (and the software that comes with it) work on your computer? Check to see if the operating system (such as Windows or Mac OSX) is listed on the camera box.

High-End Point-and-Shoot

The camera will probably have a connection port for hooking it up to the computer when you want to DOWNLOAD your pictures. This port must match your computer. USB and FIREWIRE are good ports for transferring infor-mation between computer and camera.

If your camera has removable memory cards or sticks, you can hook up a card reader (instead of the camera) to the computer.

SLR

FOCUS-FREE OR AUTOFOCUS?

Most cameras are autofocusing, and this is good. Don't confuse the terms FIXED-FOCUS or FOCUS-FREE with AUTOFOCUSING (AF) cameras. Fixed-focus or focus-free cameras are generally the least expensive, because they don't have autofocusing capability. Instead, they are designed to produce okay results as long as your subject is at a certain distance away from your camera.

Far better are the AUTOFOCUSING (AF) cameras, because they actually determine how far away the subject is from the camera. Better cameras accomplish this quickly, so there is little or no delay between the time you push the shutter button and when the camera takes the picture.

FIXED OR ZOOM LENS?

The lens on your digital camera is very important. Some cameras have a FIXED LENS, meaning you look through the viewfinder and see the scene. Then to get a wider view of the scene, you'd have to step back. To get a closer look, you'd need to step forward.

What is MB?

MB is a megabyte, which equals 1000 kilobytes (k). It's just a number that represents how much computer memory a file takes, or its file size.

A 64 MB memory card has four times (4X) as much memory space as a 16 MB card. A 2 MB file (2000K) is 100 times bigger than a 20K file.

A ZOOM lens is much better, because you can change the view just by zooming the lens from WIDE (W) to TELE (T). It's not too much different from picking up a pair of binoculars to get a closer look at a distant baseball player.

Not only is this convenient, but there will be times when you wouldn't want to step backwards or forwards—just imagine taking pictures on the edge of the Grand Canyon, and you'll know what I mean!

ALL ZOOMS ARE NOT THE SAME

Zoom lenses vary from camera to camera in two ways. The first is how wide or how close they can get you. For the greatest range of choices, look for one that lists the biggest zoom range. For example, a 4X zoom has a greater range than a 2X zoom.

Sometimes zoom lenses are described as a "35mm film format equivalent," such as 35mm–105mm. The bigger the difference between these numbers, the better the zoom range (35mm–135mm is a better range than 35mm–70mm).

The second difference is OPTICAL ZOOM versus DIGITAL ZOOM, and it's night and day between the two! OPTICAL ZOOM is much, much better. It gets you a closer look at your subject without reducing the resolution or the image quality.

If you use DIGITAL ZOOM, you will sacrifice quality and resolution! In fact, if your camera offers digital zoom, I recommend going into the control or settings menu (see the instruction manual) and turning it off.

VIEWFINDERS & MONITORS

Most digital cameras have both a viewfinder that you raise to your eye, and a monitor that's more like a TV. Most cameras with monitors allow instant picture review, so you can make sure you got the picture you wanted. If not, you can DELETE or ERASE the picture, and try again.

Some cameras with monitors also let you compose the image by watching the monitor, instead of bringing the tiny viewfinder to your eye. This can be a lot of fun, and makes shooting at crazy angles a lot easier. (See pages 44 and 45.) But be careful—it uses up battery power a lot faster.

Bigger is better when it comes to monitors! It makes it easier to PLAYBACK your pictures and ERASE them on the fly (see pages 28 and 29). A viewfinder that allows you to see exactly what the lens sees is ideal. An electronic viewfinder or a through-the-lens (TTL) viewfinder can do this. If your camera doesn't have this, you may see a slightly different version of the scene when shooting close subjects.

REMOVABLE MEMORY

Another extremely important feature for a digital camera is where it saves the image. Some inexpensive cameras record the image internally on the camera's "hard drive."

This is all right until you reach the memory capacity of the camera. If your desktop or laptop computer is nearby, there is no problem. Simply connect via cable, infrared, or data port "dock." Then DOWNLOAD the images to the computer, SAVE them, ERASE or FORMAT the camera's memory, and start shooting again.

But you may not be able to carry around a computer with you, or you simply may not have the time to DOWNLOAD the pictures. In these cases, it's great to have a camera with one of the many types of removable memory cards or memory sticks.

Like film, you load the card or stick into the camera, record your images onto it, remove it when it's full, and replace it with a blank one to begin shooting again.

When you're ready, place the full card into a card reader (or camera) that's hooked to the computer. Then SAVE the images to the computer, ERASE the card, and shoot new pictures on the same card.

When buying extra cards, make sure you pick the right type for your camera, such as Compact Flash or Smart Media.

Cards also come in different memory sizes, such as 16 MB, 64 MB, and 512 MB. The MB (MEGABYTE) figure simply tells you how much memory the card has. A higher number means it can hold more pictures before running out of room.

EXPOSURE MODES

The simplest cameras simply choose the "best" preprogrammed exposure, with results dependent on

FEATURES	BENEFITS
1. Resolution	How many megapixels (millions of pixels) the camera can capture. Sometimes this is referred to as picture size.
2. Focus Capability	Make sure your camera autofocuses. Cheaper cameras call themselves focus-free or fixed-focus and they do NOT autofocus!
3. Removable Memory	This capability allows you switch the memory card/stick when it's full, so can keep shooting and don't have to rush to a computer to download.
4. Lens/Optical Zoom	A very important capability for designing your pictures. The wider the zoom range, the better. See pages 30 and 31 for details.
5. Digital Zoom	Digital zoom is not as good as optical zoom, because it just gets you closer by cropping the image and not optically zooming (see page 16).
6. Equivalent ISO	High "Equivalent ISO" ratings indicate that the camera has better low-light capability.
7. Flash Modes	You can achieve improved results if you camera offers specialty flash modes. See pages 34 to 38 for more details.
8. Exposure Modes	Specialty exposure modes can help you get better results with action, portrait, landscape, and close-up subjects.
9. Monitor	A monitor that allows you to playback pictures is a big benefit. Some also let you compose the image in the monitor (instead of the viewfinder).
10. Viewfinder	Some viewfinders just approximate what the camera sees, while others show you what the lens sees (called through-the-lens or ttl).

how well the camera's computers analyze the lighting. Some let you customize your exposures with EXPOSURE MODES for special situations.

EXPOSURE COMPENSATION

If you find that your pictures are too light or too dark, it could be that your camera is accidentally UNDEREXPOSING (too dark) or OVEREXPOSING (too light) the pictures in certain situations. +EV or -EV EXPOSURE COMPENSATION can correct this. Usually you'll need to use the +EV command for white or light subjects, and -EV for dark subjects.

FLASH MODES

Most cameras have a built-in flash, but they are not equal. Some digital cameras provide special FLASH MODES that can improve a lot of your pictures, and make really artsy results possible (see pages 34 to 38).

COLOR CONTROL

Color shooting modes are handy. Many cameras give you choices that include "normal" or neutral color, saturated color, black-and-white, or sepia (brownish "antique") images. If your camera don't offer these choices, you can make the same basic alterations in most photo-editing software programs.

FEATURES	BENEFITS
11. Self-Timer	You'll need a self-timer function if you want to do self-portraits! See page 27 for more details.
12. Macro Capability	Don't underestimate how much fun it is to take a close-up look at the world. Some cameras let you focus on subjects just inches away.
13. Color Modes	Color modes allow you to adjust the color of your pictures when you take them, including saturated color or "antique" (sepia) brown.
14. Movie Capability	Still pictures are great, but every once in a while it's nice to have movie/video capability. See page 39 for more information.
15. Power Supply	Digital cameras are power hogs, so check how many pictures it can take on one battery charge.
16. Accessories	A few cameras offer really cool accessories, like a special case (a housing) that lets you shoot picture pictures underwater!
17. Bundled Software	Many digital cameras come with a CD of bundled software. Look for photo-editing and printing software.
18. Connection Type	You need to match your camera (or a card reader) to one of the ports in your computer (such as USB or firewire), so you can transfer the pictures.
19. Size	Listen to Goldilocks! Some cameras are so big you won't want to carry them around. Others are so small that the controls are hard to use.
20. Price	Buy only what you need today, because by the time you need to upgrade to bigger and better, those "cutting edge" cameras will be affordable.

Scanning Prints, Film & Art

You may have older pictures taken with a film camera that you want to turn into digital photos. One of the quickest and least expensive ways to digitize your conventional photographs is to use a scanner and do it yourself. Low-priced models are available, and most offer PLUG-AND-PLAY simplicity. You simply attach the scanner to your computer via a cord, install the software, and you can get good results right out of the box.

There are four basic ways to scan:

1 PRINT (FLATBED) SCANNERS

Print or flatbed scanners look like the top portion of a photocopier machine. You lift the lid, place your print face down on the glass, and click on the SCAN command. Usually a scan window opens on your computer and "walks" you through the process. Most provide controls for CROPPING and SIZING. Some also let you adjust COLOR and CONTRAST. The scan takes a few seconds (or a few minutes for slow scanners or high-resolution images) before the image pops up on your computer. When it does, SAVE it, and you have a digital version of your photo!

BOTTOM IMAGES:
Most scanners come with software that opens a CONTROL PANEL or WINDOW to walk you through the process (bottom left).
This makes it easy to scan old prints from the family album (bottom right).

Flatbed scanners can be used for more than just prints. You can scan your drawings, report cards, or any relatively flat object.

If you're careful not to scratch the glass, you can also scan 3D objects, such as fresh flowers, jewelry, stuffed animals, or merit badges (see page 22). Try draping a dark cloth over the items to produce a dark background. Black velvet is the best because it absorbs light and will scan darker.

If your objects are hard, moist, or have sharp edges, first lay a piece of clear acetate (such as blank overhead transparencies) on the glass to form a protective layer, then position your objects.

3 ALL-IN-ONE SCANNERS

Some scanners can scan prints, artwork, *and* film. Many also function as a photocopy machine and a printer.

4 STORES & LABS

If you don't want the bother of scanning older prints and negatives yourself, or you only have a few images to scan, you can consider having them done by a store or lab. *Watch out*—it may wipe out your savings, because it's not cheap. But it is easy. You simply bring in a stack of prints, negatives, or slides, then pay your money. You'll get back a CD with digitized versions of the pictures.

ABOVE: *Flatbed scanners are great for scanning prints, artwork, and relatively flat objects.*

RIGHT: *Film scanners can scan film negatives and slides.*

2 FILM SCANNERS

Transparency or film scanners are designed to shine light through a film to copy slides and negatives during the scanning process. Often they have film holders of different sizes to accommodate strips of negatives.

This Doesn't Look Like a Camera!

WHAT CAN YOU "SHOOT" WITH YOUR SCANNER?

Anything that is relatively flat works great, like a drawing, a Girl or Boy Scouts patch, and jewelry. But you can also shoot anything that can be smushed onto the glass, like a teddy bear, your soccer uniform, or a quilting project.

If the objects are too thick and you can't close the cover, drape a piece of fabric over the top. Dark fabrics work best. A tablecloth or large shirt will do the trick. Black velvet is the very best if you want a rich background color.

CAREFUL!

Be really careful not to scratch the glass on the scanner! It's a good idea to put some thick clear plastic between hard objects and the glass. (Ask your parents if they have acetate or overhead transparency materials.) In a pinch, you can tape plastic from see-through bag or plastic wrap down on the glass.

ABOVE: *Placing a box or cloth over the scanner makes the true colors come out.*

LEFT: *With the lid open and no covering, the feathers appear translucent. Which version is "best" is a matter of opinion.*

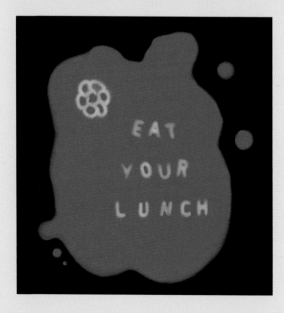

SLOPPY STUFF

You can even scan sloppy wet stuff if you put it in a very clear plastic container (like the kind berries come in). We scanned alphabet pasta and sauce. Drape cloth or an upside-down box over the container to make a dark background.

WARNING! NOTHING LIVE!

Don't be tempted to put your pet on the glass, or press your face down. The bright light is really bad for anything living.

Learn Your Camera

There are a few camera controls you'll want to learn how to use quickly and confidently. Focus Lock, Zooming, Flash, and Exposure modes will give you a lot of creative options. And it only takes a few minutes of practice to master them.

Get Focused!

Your camera might be an autofocus camera, but that doesn't mean it focuses well every time! It's kind of a stupid machine that sometimes needs your brain power to deliver great results.

Most digital cameras only know how to focus on what is in the exact center of the viewfinder. That's great, until your subject is off center.

The photo on the top of the next page is a typical portrait you might take of two friends. *But what's in the dead center of the picture?* Far away trees (as shown in the red circle). So the camera focuses on the distant trees. And if the trees are far enough away from your subjects, the people could be out of focus and look blurry in the photo.

To prevent this, you'll need to activate FOCUS LOCK. Simply center the camera on one of the subjects (such as the red circle in the center pictures), and push the shutter halfway down. When you do this, the picture won't be framed right, but don't worry. You're just telling the camera where you want it to focus. Next, without lifting your finger, swing the camera back to where you want it, and press the shutter the rest of the way down.

Check the picture in PLAYBACK mode to make sure you got it right. If you do it five or 10 times, it will become second nature and you'll soon be using FOCUS LOCK almost without thinking about it.

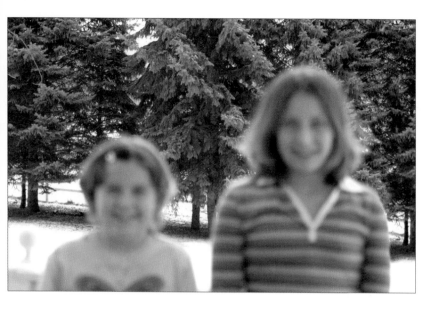

Your camera wants to focus on whatever is in the center of the frame (top images). If your subject is even a little off-center, you will need to use the Focus Lock (below).

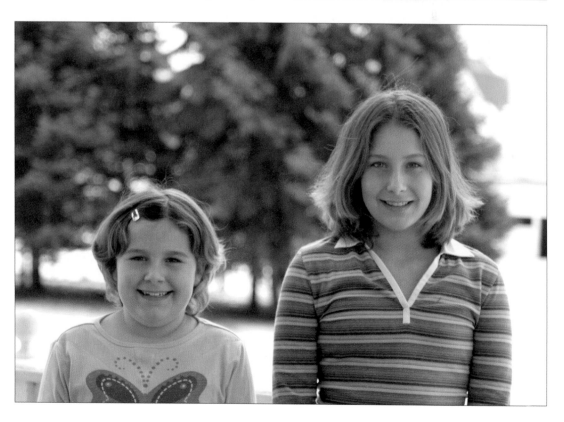

FOCUS LOCK is also helpful when shooting sports if you find your camera is too slow at autofocusing on a moving subject. Instead, you can guess where the action will be (such as home base, or the finish line in a race). Then use FOCUS LOCK to pre-focus on the right spot by pushing and holding the shutter button halfway down. When the action arrives, just push the shutter the rest of the way down, and you'll get a perfectly focused, perfectly timed picture. See page 56 for more on action shots.

Sharp Pictures

Bad focus is one way to get blurry pictures. Another is if your camera is selecting too slow a shutter speed. *What's a shutter speed?* That's the amount of time the camera needs to open up a hole (or window) in the

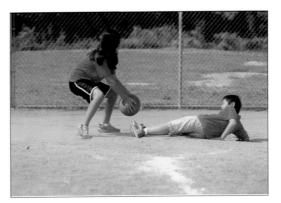

LEFT: You know where home plate is! As the runner starts for the base, pre-focus on the spot using FOCUS LOCK, and then take the picture as the action happens. You can also try panning the camera (see page 56).

lens so that light can shine through and record the scene on the camera's imaging device. A certain amount of light is needed for a proper exposure. In dim lighting, the camera must leave this hole open for a longer period of time to record the image.

Image blurring occurs if the hole is open long enough for the subject or camera to move *while* the image is being recorded.

FOUR LEFT IMAGES: In dim lighting, a picture can turn out blurry because while the picture was being taken either the camera shook, the subject moved, or both. It's not as obvious in the full version (far top left), but when it's blown up large (near top left) it looks bad.

Solutions for a sharper picture (far bottom left) include switching to a HIGHER EQUIVALENT ISO, steadying the camera (see page 27), and asking your subject to "hold still." Even when blown up large (near bottom left) it still looks sharp.

You'll rarely get blurred images on a bright sunny day, because your camera can select fast shutter speeds that "freeze" motion. But as the light gets dimmer, there's more chance that you'll accidentally get blur.

Three things can fix this:

1 MOVE INTO A BRIGHTER AREA

Improve the lighting by opening up window blinds, turning on the room lights, or moving outdoors.

2 TURN ON THE FLASH

Add light by turning on our camera's built-in flash. (See pages 34 to 38.)

3 A HIGHER EQUIVALENT ISO

Select a higher number EQUIVALENT ISO if it is available on your camera.

Equivalent ISO

Some cameras offer an EQUIVALENT ISO setting. This is similar to the ISO ratings of film, and indicates their low-light capability (with a higher number being better). On some cameras it can be set to AUTOMATIC, 100, 200, 400, and sometimes higher.

If you're shooting in low light and your shots are blurry, switch to a higher number setting. This will help you get sharper images, but it will reduce the overall quality, so when you move back into brighter light, remember to put it back to the lower number or to AUTO.

Get in the Picture!

Sometimes it's no fun being the one taking the pictures because you're not in them. Well, most cameras offer a SELF-TIMER, usually indicated by a symbol of a clock or stopwatch. When you activate the SELF-TIMER and then press the shutter button, the SELF-TIMER will delay the picture-taking for 10 or 15 seconds. If you're clever, you can place the camera on a solid object such as a table, hit the SELF-TIMER, and then run around to get in front of the lens, so you're in the picture too.

The best way to steady your camera is with a tripod. They come in big, expensive models, as well as in inexpensive pocket sizes. With a pocket tripod, you simple open the legs, screw on the camera (there should be a screw thread on the bottom), place it on a steady table or other object of the right height, and shoot.

You can also come up with novel solutions, such as nestling your camera in a coat or on top of a bag of rice.

Warning! Some cameras will focus on the scene when you first activate the SELF-TIMER, so it could misfocus on the background instead of you and your friends (see pages 24 and 25). If you find this happening, pick a spot that's against a wall, or have your friends stand in the center of the frame, and then try again.

Why Use Playback?

Most digital cameras will let you review your pictures in PLAYBACK mode after you take them. You can scroll through the pictures in the memory one at a time. Often you can view four, nine, or 16 images at a time if you want to locate a particular picture quickly.

A nice feature is the ability to MAGNIFY each image by pushing a symbol of a magnifying glass with a + (magnify) or - (shrink) marking. You can use it to see the details of the picture, such as if your subject has a good expression or if the subject is in focus.

CONSERVING BATTERIES

The only reason to turn off the monitor is if you're worried about battery power. One of the quickest ways to run down the batteries is to view the scene with the monitor, and play it back to watch afterwards. If you're worried about stretching your battery power, use the viewfinder to shoot pictures, and wait to view the pictures.

Also check the menu settings to see if the post-picture "review" (usually two seconds) can be turned off. You'll find you can take a lot more pictures before having to change or recharge the batteries.

Trash It!

Don't be afraid to DELETE or ERASE pictures that aren't very good. They fill up the memory, and you'll waste time transferring them into the computer. This includes out of focus images or pictures that don't look good. The MAGNIFY button (see above) will help you check the details.

The ERASE control (sometimes called DELETE or TRASH) is usually indicated by a symbol of a garbage can. Be careful to read the MENU when you use the ERASE feature, because you can erase a single picture or *all* the pictures in the memory.

BELOW: *most cameras allow you to PLAYBACK your photos after you take them. Some let you view multiple pictures at a time to quickly locate an image (left), full frame (center) or magnified (right).*

LEFT: *Some of the buttons on a digital camera control different functions depending on whether you're in* SHOOTING *mode or* PLAYBACK *mode. On this camera, the right-hand buttons control the lens zooming (*WIDE *or* TELE*) in shooting mode, and magnification of the* PLAYBACK *when reviewing photos.*

ABOVE: *The symbol of a garbage can allows you to* ERASE *images you have already shot.*

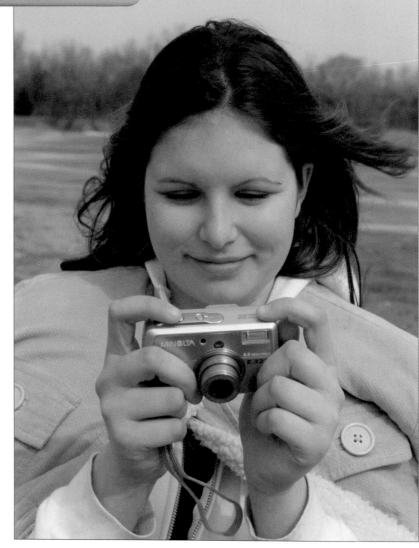

RIGHT: *Being able to review your pictures moments after you take them is one of the best features of a digital camera.*

Cameras with Zoom

Zoom lenses are a great feature, because without moving your feet you can dramatically change what's included in the picture. By zooming to the TELE or T setting, you can "get closer" to your subject. At the WIDE or W setting, you can include more of the scene in front of you, which is really helpful when you're trying to fit a bunch of people into the image.

OPTICAL OR DIGITAL?

The best kind of zoom is OPTICAL ZOOM. Optical means that the lens changes so that the image is magnified as you go from wide to tele. This delivers much higher quality images than DIGITAL ZOOM, which magnifies the image by cropping and enlarging the center portion. This in effect reduces the resolution and therefore the quality.

The only benefit of DIGITAL ZOOM is that it saves time later because you won't have to crop the image in photo-editing software to make it look bigger. In general, turn off the DIGITAL ZOOM, and just use the OPTICAL ZOOM if available. Walk closer to the subject if you want it bigger.

Wide

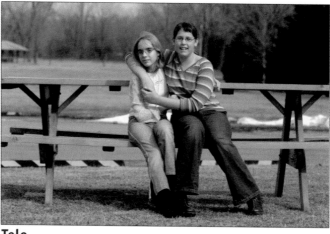

Tele

Zooming isn't just for making your subjects bigger. It can also change how they look. In the above images, the photographer moved to keep the girls the same size in both the wide and tele modes. Look below to compare how the background (and the tree) changed.

Background Check

Your zoom lens setting can have a huge affect on the final look of your photograph. A WIDE lens setting was chosen for the first picture (above left), then the TELE setting (above right). In the WIDE version, the photographer was just a few feet away from the subjects, and the two girls fill the frame.

When the photographer switched to the TELE zoom setting, at that same distance the photo would only have showed their heads. So the photographer stepped back until the two girls fit into the photograph (from head to toe) and took the picture.

Notice the difference in how the girls look. The TELE setting is probably the most flattering. But the biggest difference is the background. The girls didn't move an inch, yet the trees in the TELE version now looks huge, and you can't see any sky.

Pretty cool, huh? Try experimenting by moving closer and farther away from your subject, while zooming the camera to keep them about the same size in the picture. For more information on backgrounds, see pages 51 to 55.

Background looks small

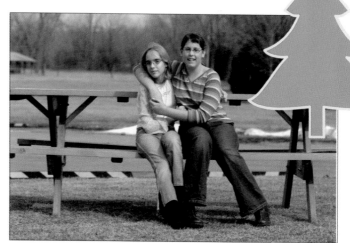

Background looks huge

Making Funny Faces...

Both lens settings & software create fun distortions.

The TELE or T setting on your zoom camera is the BEST choice for portraits if you want the person to look his or her best (see page 41). However, if you want to get a little crazy and create some distortions, read on!

THIS PAGE: *Shooting from a distance with the TELE lens setting may make you look the best (above), but getting close and WIDE sure is perfect if you're determined to goof it up for the camera.*

RIGHT:
Photo-editing software can be used to create entertaining distortions of your images.

WIDE-ANGLE LENS SETTING

For the most dramatic lens effects, set the camera to the WIDE or W lens setting, and move close to your subject.

You'll need to learn your camera's minimal focusing distance to make sure your results are sharp. Some cameras will beep or shine a light in the viewfinder if you are too close. Others will refuse to shoot. You can always read the instruction manual to find out how close you can get.

Or just try it, and then check the monitor playback. Use the MAGNIFICATION option to blow up the picture on the monitor so you can really check the focus. (If your camera has this option, it will usually be activated by the button with a magnifying glass with the symbols "+" or "–" inside.)

SOFTWARE DISTORTIONS

Some photo-editing and specialty software (like Kai's SuperGoo) let you quickly create silly distortions of your photographs—like bug eyes and pinched faces (above).

For the most dramatic effects, start with lens distortion (far left) and then add software distortions (below).

RIGHT:
Try combining lens distortion with software distortion for the wildest results!

News Flash!

When you're indoors or the lighting is dim, your camera may not be able to take sharp pictures because there's not enough light. The result is a big blur.

However, some cameras will automatically add flash, so you have enough light to get an unblurry picture. On other cameras, you may have to manually push a button or pop up the flash.

REALITY CHECK

The small, built-in flash on most point-and-shoot cameras is not very powerful. It's important to understand the limitations of this flash in terms of the range of distances where it works well. If you're too close (a few feet), then the subject may be too brightly lit because the camera can't reduce the flash's power enough.

If you're too far away, then it can't reach far enough and the subject will be dark. A good example of this would be an evening baseball game. The camera wants to light up the distant ball players, but you'd need huge stadium lights to do that! Check the instruction manual for the flash range on your camera.

Flash requires a lot of battery power, and it can sometimes take a few seconds for the flash to recharge. Depending on the camera, the camera may refuse to shoot again until the flash is ready, or it may take the picture anyway at less than full power (probably resulting in a subject that's too dark). Check your instruction manual so you'll know when it's safe to shoot again.

If your batteries are getting weak, the camera may still be able to take pictures but not have enough strength to fully power the flash. This could happen even if the "low battery" symbol might not yet be showing.

FLASH MODES

Some digital cameras have special FLASH MODES that let you get better pictures or create crazy effects.

1 AUTOFLASH

This is the camera's automatic flash mode. If the camera thinks the lighting is too dark, it will automatically fire the flash. Sometimes this might not be what you want, in which case you can select FLASH OFF (see page 36).

2 RED-EYE REDUCTION FLASH

Red-eye is that annoying "devilish" red color that fills the eyes of some people in flash pictures.

RED-EYE REDUCTION FLASH mode causes a bright lamp or series of flashes to go off before you actually take pictures, reducing this effect.

Unfortunately, this can be annoying and causes a delay before the picture is taken. Your subjects may not have red-eye, but they could have a startled look or may have already looked away because they thought the pre-flash was the picture moment.

Instead, you can risk producing the red-eye effect, and then improve it on the computer later. Easy RED-EYE repair functions are found in some photo-editing software, such as Microsoft Picture It or MGI PhotoSuite.

BELOW: Red-eye sometimes occurs when photographing people in dim lighting. It can be reduced or eliminated using RED-EYE REDUCTION FLASH *mode or in photo-editing software on the computer.*

It's not Halloween! So why did she get those red demon eyes?

3 FILL-FLASH

FILL FLASH is the quickest way to make significant improvements in many of your outdoor pictures. In bright, sunny situations, the sun can cause deep shadows on the faces of your subjects that hide their features.

The AUTOFLASH feature on most cameras fires when the lighting gets dim. FILL FLASH, on the other hand, forces the flash to fire even in these bright situations. The flash then fills the shadow without having a major effect on the main light (the sun).

It also adds attractive highlights to your subject's eyes. Because this feature makes such a significant improvement in your pictures, when in doubt, use it!

4 NIGHT (OR SLOW) FLASH

Occasionally, you'll want to take a backlit or nighttime portrait with an interesting background, such as city lights or the last glimmer of a sunset.

If your camera has NIGHT FLASH mode (sometimes called SLOW SYNC flash), this is a good time to use it. NIGHT FLASH mode combines a flash exposure (which illuminates a nearby subject) with a longer shutter speed (see page 26) to get a good picture.

For optimal results, steady the camera with a tripod or brace it against a solid object to keep the background sharp.

5 FLASH OFF

Most cameras will automatically fire the flash if the light is dim (AUTOFLASH mode). Sometimes natural lighting can be wonderful by itself, such as at dawn or dusk. If this is the case, you may want to overrule the camera's setting and turn the flash off. Usually this mode is indicated by a symbol of a lighting bolt symbol and the "no" circle-and-slash symbol around it.

If you choose FLASH OFF in low-light or dimmer lighting situations, your camera will be using a relatively slow shutter speed.

(Continued on page 38.)

LEFT: *Turn the flash off for candles, jack o'lanterns, fireworks, and neon signs.*

Nasty Shadows Ruining Your Pictures?

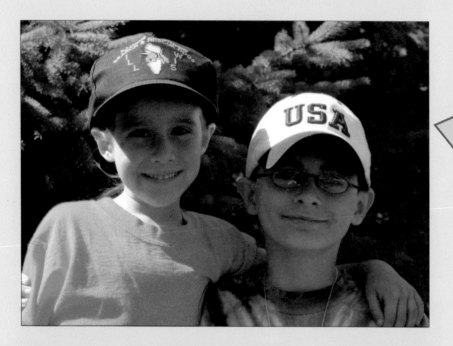

In bright sunlight, your camera doesn't "think" it needs to add light by firing the flash. However, sunlight can cause dark shadows on the faces of your subjects, especially if they're wearing hats with visors or brims.

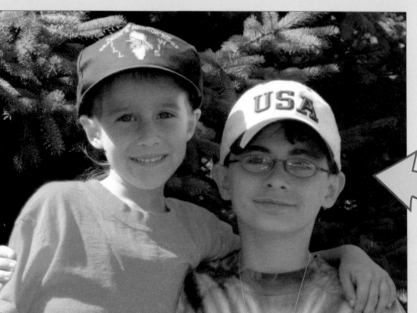

But you're smarter than the camera! When you see dark shadows on the faces of your subjects, turn on the FILL-FLASH feature. This will lighten the shadows, without affecting other parts of the picture very much. The higher the sun is in the sky, the longer and darker the shadows will be. So high noon is the perfect time for FILL-FLASH.

This can cause the picture to be blurred unless you steady the camera (see pages 26 and 27).

You can do this by using a tripod, bracing it on a steady object, or snuggling it in a coat or towel. Switching to a higher EQUIVALENT ISO on your digital camera will also help you get sharper results (see page 27).

FLASH OFF can also be used for candles, such as a birthday cake or a jack o'lantern. A candle can sometimes produce enough light for a cool-looking picture. Set the camera to FLASH OFF or you'll ruin the effect by over-powering the candle's light with the flash (see the examples below).

Flash On vs. Flash Off

Trying Flash Off? Hold the camera very steady or you'll end up with a blur.

The camera fires the flash (AUTOFLASH mode) because the lighting is dim.

FLASH OFF mode, but the camera or subject moved causing blurring.

FLASH OFF mode, but this time the camera is held steady and the subject stayed still.

Exposure Modes

Some high-end cameras offer special EXPOSURE MODES that help the camera perform in certain situations.

The most common EXPOSURE MODE is the PROGRAM (P) or AUTOMATIC mode. This is the fully automated mode of the camera. It will set the camera controls for the average subject, making it a good choice for everyday snapshots. Some cameras only offer this mode.

BELOW: Some cameras offer an ACTION mode for shooting fast-moving subjects.

PORTRAIT exposure mode is, not surprisingly, a great choice for portraits. This mode tells the camera to try to throw the background out of focus so the emphasis is on your subject.

An out-of-focus background tends to be most attractive in portraiture because it eliminates distractions in the background that would take away from the impact of the main subject. Your camera CONTROL DIAL or LCD PANEL may have a symbol of a head-and-shoulders to indicate this mode.

BOTTOM RIGHT: Many digital cameras have close-focusing capability. Some even offer a CLOSE-UP or MACRO mode.

ACTION mode sets the camera so that the shutter speed is as fast as possible. This will result in the sharpest (least blurred) result.

MACRO or CLOSE-UP mode, usually depicted by a flower symbol, optimizes the camera for shooting small subjects up close.

Movie Mode

A few cameras have a MOVIE mode that takes short movies instead of still photographs. Usually they are fairly low resolution and last under a minute. Some cameras create silent movies, while other record sound.

The more FRAMES-PER-SECOND (fps) the camera boasts, the smoother the action will be. Movies done at 10 or 15 fps can look very jerky.

Take Great Pictures

Once you know how to operate your camera, you can start taking snapshots. However, if you want to move from "just plain snapshots" to really great pictures, you'll want to check out some of these easy techniques.

The term COMPOSITION is a word that's often used to describe how a picture or painting is designed. You may instinctively know that one picture looks better than many of your other snapshots, but it might not be easy to figure out exactly why. Most of the photos you really like probably have good COMPOSITIONS. Pinpointing what makes a composition good or bad can be a challenge.

The tips and techniques shown in this chapter should help you figure this out by helping you design better photographs (and therefore create better compositions). Once you know why certain techniques improve your pictures, then they can all be winners.

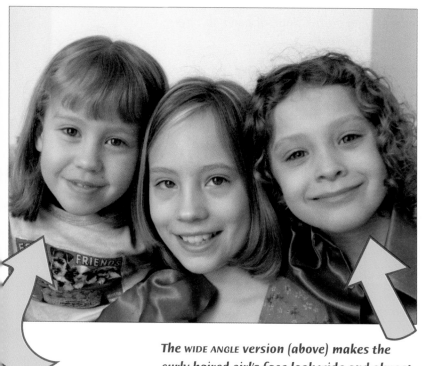

Zoooooom to Tele for Portraits

When you shoot portraits with a WIDE zoom lens setting, the picture gets distorted. You might not realize it, but the photo will somehow seem less pleasing and your subject may even look "fat." The closer you get to the subject and the closer to WIDE the lens setting, the weirder it looks.

For a flattering portrait, step back and zoom all the way out to the TELE or T setting. Then step back until you have the composition you want. Usually for portraits, this means a head-and-shoulders picture. If space is limited, do the best you can.

The combination of a WIDE lens setting, and a close shooting distance makes the girl on the left look younger than she really is by distorting her face. Because younger kids tend to have larger, chubbier faces (compared to their bodies), the lens distortion makes this girl look younger than she is!

In the version to the right, she looks closer to how she looks in person. It was shot from farther away with the lens zoomed to the TELE setting.

The WIDE ANGLE version (above) makes the curly haired girl's face look wide and almost comical. The version below (shot farther away with the TELE setting) is more flattering.

SEEING EYE TO EYE

My favorite portraiture trick is simple. Determine your subject's eye level and raise or lower yourself to the same level.

Most people shoot at their own standing eye level and rarely change to different levels. This is fine and dandy if every friend and family member you have is your *exact* height. But what about shorter siblings? You'll be looking down on them. Or taller parents? You'll be looking up at them. And how about people sitting on chairs, lying on the floor, or hanging from the monkey bars?

Try to match their height to take the picture, even if it means getting down on your knees or stepping up on a stool. It may sound like a lot of extra effort, but you'll be amazed in the difference it can make in your portraits.

The chart below will help get you started, But the basic rule is to think about your height *before* you shoot. It may sound simple, but it really works. Then check out pages 44 and 45 for exceptions to the rule!

Subject Type	Shooting Position
Same Height Friend	Shoot from your normal standing position.
People Who Are Taller than You	Stand on a chair, a step, or even your tip-toes.
Standing Toddler	You're taller than a two-year-old, so get on your knees or squat low.
Sitting Person or Pet on Chair	Sit on a chair across from the subject, or squat to a sitting height.
Person or Pet Lying on the Ground	Get down on the ground, so you'll be at their eye level.
Unusual Angle	*Look up! Look down!* Position yourself or your subject high or low, such as on a balcony, cliff, or edge of a pool.

Lying on the ground and looking up at the photographer is not a very comfortable position. It also creates an odd and confusing angle.

Compare this to when the photographer also lies down on the floor. Not only is the photograph more flattering, but it's more friendly.

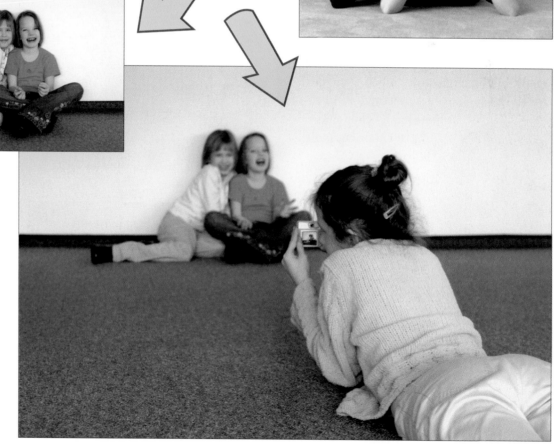

Break the Rules!

It's easy to get stuck in a rut—go high & low for crazy angles.

PLAY THE ANGLES!

Most snapshots are taken from the photographer's eye level while standing. As described on pages 42 and 43, this is not usually the best angle for portraits of people who are lower or higher than your eye level. Many of these pictures can be improved by changing that shooting angle.

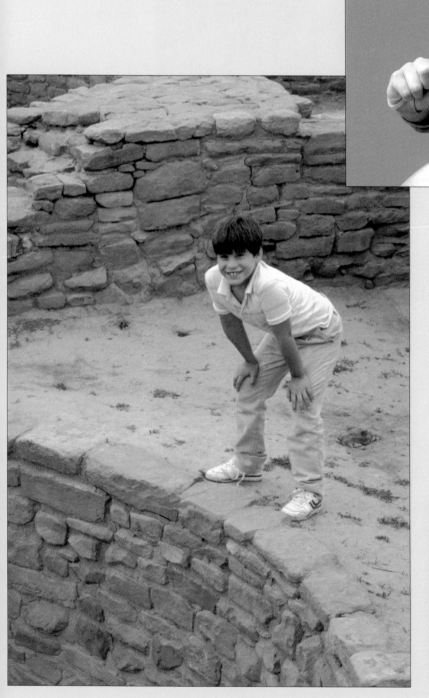

Since we spend our lives seeing the world from our own eye level, standing shots are the most common angle of view. You can really shake things up by getting down low or up high to shoot a picture.

Try lying on the ground or shooting down from a stairwell. And when everyone else is looking straight ahead, try looking up or down.

You can exaggerate your new perspective by coming in close with a wide-angle lens or zooming in from far away.

Gotcha!

Portraits of your friends smiling at the camera are fine, but after a while they can get kind of boring. Some of the most successful photos of people are taken when the subject isn't paying attention to your camera.

CARRY YOUR CAMERA

Start by remembering to carry your camera with you on a regular basis. You just never know when your friends are going to start doing something fun or interesting. When they do, just casually take out your camera and take the photo without making a fuss.

ZOOM TO TELE

If your camera has a zoom lens, you can zoom to the TELE or T setting. This will allow you to shoot frame-filling pictures from a

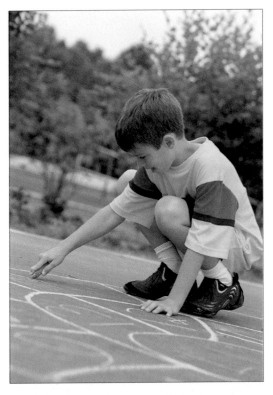

LEFT: Stealth and using the monitor to shoot from the hip will help you get great candid pictures of your friends doing cool stuff.

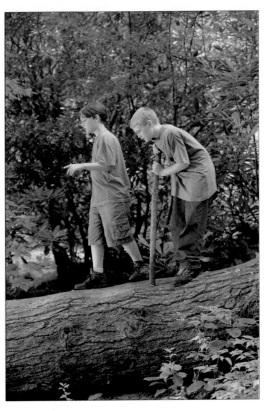

LEFT: Exploring is a great time to carry your camera!

RIGHT: *Digital pictures are free, so take a lot. You can erase all the bad ones—you just need one good one!*

distance. The further away from your subject you can get, the less likely they will notice what you're doing.

USE THE MONITOR
Some digital cameras have the advantage of a monitor that lets you compose the picture without having to bring the camera to your eye. Not only is this convenient, but you can be very sneaky about your photography— *regular spy stuff!* The more you practice, the better you'll get at "shooting from the hip" to get great unposed (candid) pictures.

BRATTY BROTHER SYNDROME
Mastering the monitor will also come in handy if your little brother keeps being a

goof in shot after shot after shot. Don't give up. Just make him think you're not ready to take the picture, by moving the camera further away from your eye and face. Then just take quick peeks to make sure you're pointed in the right direction. When he *finally* acts normal, you can click off the picture! Luckily it's digital, so you can DELETE, DELETE, DELETE the bad versions.

This works great for pets too. If you have a dog, you've probably noticed that every time you point the camera in his direction, he comes running over because he thinks you're looking at him. But if you hold the camera low and look down at the monitor, you'll have a lot less trouble.

Everyone Say, "Cheese!"

Photographing a group of people is actually a difficult thing to do well. For starters, just shooting everyone smiling and with their eyes open can be tough. Here are some hints:

1 TAKE A LOT OF PICTURES

The only insurance is to take a lot of pictures and hope that everyone's eyes are open and hope for the best. If you take five or six shots, you have a much better chance.

2 AVOID THE LINE-UP SHOT

Beyond taking a zillion pictures, the next trick is to get creative with the posing. Usually, your first instinct will be to line up everyone with their shoulders next to each other for the picture. This is rarely the best composition, and you end up with a picture that looks like a police line-up.

3 SOME IN FRONT, SOME BEHIND

Instead, just try to put the heads at different heights. This makes the composition more exciting. It also has the added bonus of

BELOW:
Compare the line-up pictures on the bottom left, with the version where every one is on a picnic bench and their heads are at different levels. Not only do these look better, but you can see their faces better because they are larger (compare the yellow oval sizes).

tightening the group so you can move or zoom in closer to make the faces larger.

The simplest way is the "sports team" photo pose. To do this is to make several rows, with the front line sitting, kneeling, or even lying down. Seat your parents (or an especially tall or short person) so they don't stick out from the group.

4 THE STACKING OR STAIR METHOD

Instead of rows, you can use a staircase, picnic bench, or boulder to put people at different heights so everyone's face is fully visible in the picture.

5 SOFTWARE COMBINATIONS

Perhaps the most entertaining method is to shoot separate images of different people and combine them into one picture using STITCHING or COLLAGING software.

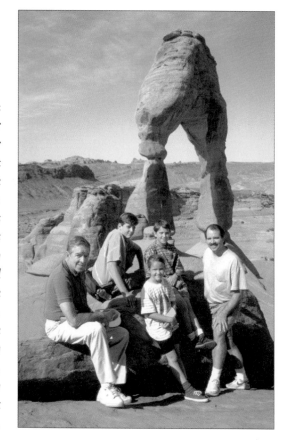

RIGHT IMAGES:
Try to "stack" your subjects so their heads are at different levels and they're grouped more closely. Not only does this look better, but it lets you make them bigger in the final photo (previous page and far right images). Or it gives you the room to show a dramatic background, like Delicate Arch in Arches National Park (near right).

Off-Centered

When designing your pictures, your first instinct will probably be to center your subject in the center of the viewfinder like a bull's eye target. However, this is rarely the best photograph.

A handy guideline is to put the main subject off to the side, instead of in the dead center of the frame. It's sometimes called the RULE OF THIRDS because the best place to position the subject is along the outer third of the photo.

To understand the RULE OF THIRDS, draw an imaginary tic-tac-toe board over the picture (bottom left image), and place the subject along one of the lines. Notice how the boy and girl are along the left line, and the boy's face is on the intersection point.

In the comparison shown at the bottom right, the straight portrait has the boy's face smack in the center. But by moving him off to the side, the picture has a stronger design.

Experienced photographers often take it to further extremes, placing subjects even farther away from the center of the frame than the guideline of one-third.

This doesn't mean your main subject always has to be off center, but quite often, it is the best choice. This is especially true if the background helps to tell the story of the picture (see pages 54 and 55).

When shooting an off-center composition, be sure to use the FOCUS LOCK function, or your subject may be out of focus. See pages 24 and 25 for details.

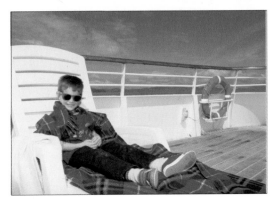

RIGHT: *Moving your main subject off to one side often improves the picture.*

LEFT: *The yellow lines in the far bottom left picture demonstrate how the subjects are placed along one of the lines that divides the picture into thirds.*

Creating Better Backgrounds

THIS PAGE: *Okay, okay, the "photo" below is a joke. But it serves to show how colors, words, and clutter can rob the attention from your main subject! Compare this to the photo on the right.*

One of the quickest ways to wreck a good picture is to have a bad background. You may be so excited about the subject in front of you that you completely ignore what's behind.

The main subject is great, so who cares about the background? Unfortunately, when you enlarge your pictures, you'll care. Suddenly the picture doesn't look half as good as it did

in the viewfinder or on the monitor. *Why?* Because when you were taking the picture, you had "tunnel vision." All you saw was the subject at the end of the tunnel, and not everything else around it. But later, when you or your friends look at the picture, this other non-subject stuff will look terrible. Whoever is looking at the picture will be distracted by unimportant elements in the picture.

REMOVE THE CLUTTER
You clean up your room *(sometimes)*, so why not "clean up" your photos too? Try to minimize background clutter and avoid distracting elements (see page 55).

WATCH FOR ANTLERS
Poles, trees and other vertical objects in the background may look like they're "growing" out of your subject's head like the antlers of a deer. Just a step to the right or left can often shift them in relation to your subject.

READ ME NOW!!
I AM MORE IMPORTANT
THAN THE PERSON

AVOID BRIGHT HIGHLIGHTS

Bright areas in the background tend to draw the viewer's attention away from the subject. Watch out for reflection off metal and bright lights.

GOOD COLORS, WRONG PLACE

Bold colors (like red or yellow) can also be distracting if they appear as spots in the background.

LEAVE OUT YOUR ABC'S

Words and text, such as signs and billboards almost *beg* to be read. If they say something important to the story of the picture (see pages 54 and 55), you can leave them in. But if not, you're better off getting rid of them.

What would be a sign you might leave in a picture? Leave in the "Dr. Smith's Dentistry" sign when you take a picture of your sister with her nice straight teeth on the day her braces come off!

CROOKED CAMERA

A picture that was taken with the camera held crookedly will cause the background to look as if it's sliding to one side or the other, as if you were on a sinking ship. Luckily this is easy to fix in the computer by rotating the image to straighten the background.

Improve Your Backgrounds

Now you know what makes a background bad, but what's the cure? Take the picture, and then very carefully look for the following previously mentioned background problems that can spoil an otherwise good potential picture.

The picture shown of puppies sitting on somebody's lap (far left picture) is an example of a

bad background choice. The cut-off head makes you want to ask, "*Who is that person?*" Plus, the colorful T-shirt design makes the background very distracting.

You can avoid many of the background problems by performing one or more of these actions:

1 Move the subjects so they are positioned against a less cluttered background. Here, the tired pups were placed on the floor and then repositioned when they were soundly asleep.

2 Zoom in with the TELE setting (or step closer) to fill more of the frame with the subject, thereby eliminating more of the background distractions (the bottom of the couch and chair in this case).

3 Move to the left, right, up or down to change your angle, so the background changes in relation to the subject.

4 Use photo-editing software to retouch a cluttered background or remove a distracting object. You can also use photo-editing software to crop the image so that the subject is more prominent and the background is no longer part of the image.

Tell a Story

The old proverb states: "A picture is worth a thousand words." *But not every picture!* It's up to you, the photographer, to decide what story to tell with each photograph, and how many words it will be worth.

Many of the tips in this book have emphasized filling the frame with the all-important subject. However, sometimes it's better to include more of the background. A portrait is a portrait after all. But a picture can also tell the story of an event, such as cutting down the perfect Christmas tree.

If the background helps tell the story of the photograph, such as this family trip to an ancient ruin (right), include it so the person viewing your picture will get a good look at the surroundings.

Zoom the camera lens to the WIDE setting to get as much of the scene in the picture as possible. If your camera doesn't have a zoom, step back as far as you can.

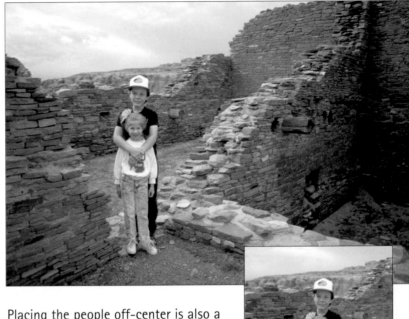

Placing the people off-center is also a good idea, because it usually produces a better COMPOSITION. (See page 50 for more details on off-centered pictures.) If your subjects aren't in the middle, be sure to use FOCUS LOCK before shooting the picture. (See pages 24 and 25 for information on FOCUS LOCK.)

THIS PAGE: *The backgrounds in the top and bottom photos are important parts of these pictures, because they tell us about a trip to a ruin (top) or that the boy has just chopped down this Christmas tree (left). The middle shot of just the brother and sister is a simple portrait, but reveals almost nothing about where they are.*

A big maroon chair and the radiator in the background attract our eye.

A pile of books adds no important information to the picture, but instead makes the room looked more cluttered, and the picture confusing.

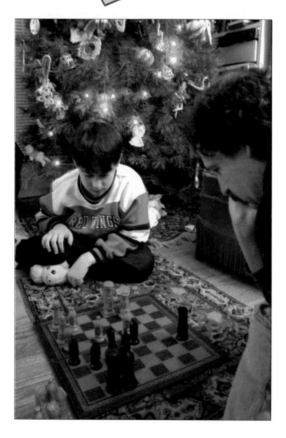

Careful! Not *Too* Much Background!

Often there will be *too* much stuff in the background for a good picture, and you'll need to simplify it. Determine which elements are important to your picture and eliminate the rest.

The image above contains a lot of distracting items that don't tell the story of this Christmas chess showdown. The arrows point to a cluttered bookcase, a maroon chair, and a bright red plastic cup.

To create a better background, the photographer chose a different shooting angle for the photo on the left. At first glance, the Christmas tree in the background could be considered distracting, because of the bright colored lights. However, it's an important part of the picture because it tells us that it's Christmas.

Catch the Action

For the best looking pictures of a moving subject (especially one that's moving from left to right, or right to left), you should PAN your camera. Basically, this means you follow the subject in the viewfinder before, during, and after you take the photograph.

In general, this will result in the sharpest action pictures. When the light is too dim for sharp photos of fast-moving subjects, the panning technique will help you get artistically blurred pictures.

To pan, stand with your feet slightly apart and both hands holding the camera. Then, twist your upper body and hips without moving your feet, while keeping the subject centered in the viewfinder or monitor. Try not to bob up and down, and keep the motion as smooth as possible.

If you find you're missing the peak of the action, it may be because your camera is slow to focus. If this is the case, push the shutter slightly before the perfect moment. Or use FOCUS LOCK (see pages 24 and 25) to pre-focus on the spot your subject will pass.

Perfect panning pictures take practice. Stand on the sidewalk and practice on passing cars or bicycles. Once you've mastered panning, you'll be amazed at how great your action shots look.

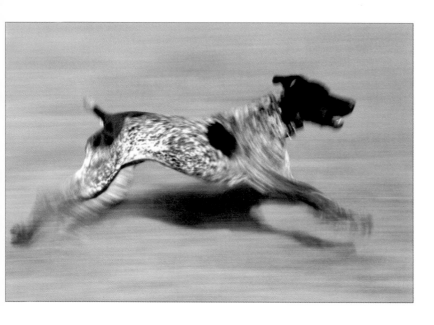

FAR LEFT: *This action photo is sharp because the photographer used the panning technique described on the previous page. Even on bright days, you may need to pan to get sharp images of fast subjects.*

NEAR LEFT: *Dim light prevented a sharp image of this running dog. However, panning saved the day by making it an artistic image.*

Notice how the dog is relatively sharp, when compared to the background. This is because the panning kept the dog sort of still (centered) in the viewfinder during the long exposure, while the background changed (and thus blurred). Legs go back and forth and heads bob more than the torso of the dog, so these are more blurred.

BOTTOM: *Proper panning requires that you track the subject in the viewfinder as it moves across the scene in front of you. Keep your feet planted and swing your hips in a smooth motion while keeping the subject in the center of the viewfinder.*

Fun Ideas & Projects

Armed with your digital camera, an inkjet printer, and a few supplies, you can create a wide variety of crafts. Start with these and springboard to your own ideas!

Change Your Change Purse!

Use t-shirt transfer paper to *change* a change purse into something really cool. Start by selecting a fabric purse and some fabric transfer paper. Some transfer papers are done cold, but others require a heated iron. If heat is required, make sure the purse's fabric won't melt!

You can either scan the coins (see pages 20 and 21) or photograph them with your digital camera.

For the latter, spread loose change over a clean area such as a sheet or floor. Try not to have any blank spaces between the coins. Do it near a window or in a fairly bright area so you won't need a flash, because the flash could cause glare off the metal coins.

Transfer the picture to your computer and save it. Measure the area of your purse to be covered. Use a PRINTING TEMPLATE, WORD-PROCESSING software, or PHOTO-EDITING software to print the picture.

You may want to do a print on regular paper first, to check the size before using the expensive transfer paper. When you have it right, print the transfer paper, trim it carefully and apply it to the purse following the instructions that come with the paper.

Pet Portraits

The basic concept to this project is to bend a wire coat hanger into a square shape, cover it with fabric, and decorate it with hot or cold t-shirt transfer material.

Begin by taking a good digital shot of your pet. Then select some pet-oriented objects like biscuits, squeak toys or a collar and scan them (see pages 20 and 21). Look for free funny CLIPART as well. (CLIPART is available on CDs, as well as for free from some websites. Do an Internet search under the words "free clipart" to find sources.)

You can COLLAGE the pet picture with the other objects to make one photo. Or you can print and transfer them separately.

Reshape the hanger into a rectangle, and measure the size. You want your picture (or pictures) to be under this size. Print the picture on the transfer paper.

Cut out all the iron-on pieces with the scissors. Cut a piece of patterned fabric a little smaller than the opening in the hanger. Transfer the pet portrait onto this fabric. Be sure to follow the iron-on paper's instructions for how to do it.

To make the frame, lay the reshaped hanger onto a larger piece of canvas, and cut the canvas 2 inches bigger than the outside edges of the hanger. Round off the corners and cut a few lines at the corners so it will wrap around smoothly.

Turn the canvas face down and center the hanger in the middle of the canvas. Cover the hanger's handle with a paper towel. Spray the outside 2 inches of the canvas with spray adhesive, or you can apply white glue. Neatly turn the edges over the hanger. Wrap the hanger's handle with a piece of yarn.

Glue the fabric with the picture onto the canvas frame. For added flare, cut a triangle of bandanna fabric. Iron on some small pictures. Tie a knot in two ends of the triangle.

WHAT YOU NEED

- Digital photo of your pet
- Scans, digital photos, or clipart of pet-related objects such as toys
- Wire coat hanger
- 12x18-inch piece of lightweight canvas
- 8x10-inch scrap of patterned cotton fabric.
- Bandanna material
- Spray adhesive or white glue
- Iron-on transfer paper (hot or cold transfer depending on the fabric)
- Very sharp scissors
- 12-inch piece of yarn

Simple Stationery

The simplest photo stationary uses pictures to make a border around the writing space on a piece of paper. You can mix your own photos with CLIPART cartoons, borders, and words.

In Photo Software

You can design your stationery in most photo-editing software, such as Adobe Photoshop Elements, MGI PhotoSuite, Microsoft Picture It, Scansoft PhotoFactory, and Ulead PhotoImpact.

Remember that you can use photos, as well as other tools like the PAINTBRUSH (which made the blue stripes in the example shown below). Better software gives you hundreds of choices in BRUSH types and size, as well as COLOR, SHADE, and the PATTERN it makes.

The yellow diamond shapes were made by creating an AUTO SHAPE and then filling or painting it with color. Some programs have special FILTERS or BRUSH effects to add texture or patterns to these shapes. A diamond shape was used for the yellow at the top of the page.

Letter-Weight Papers

For the best results, use papers made for ink-jet printing. You don't need the glossy, expensive photo-weight papers. These will be hard to fold anyway. Instead pick something in the 20 to 27lb. range.

The instructions will vary depending on what software you use.

In Word Software

You can also design your stationery in word processing software, such as Microsoft Word. To do this, you will have to first gather all your elements in photo software (see above), and select INSERT→PICTURE→FROM FILE to place the elements. The WordArt function in some versions of Microsoft Word allows you to create crazy type as well.

Last Step

The last step is easy! Print the picture. Use scissors to follow edges of a picture or shape (such as the yellow diamonds) for a special look. Crafts scissors that make a scalloped or jagged edge are also fun.

Transparency Option

Some photo software programs let you change the TRANSPARENCY or OPACITY of the picture or a LAYER or portion of the picture. This is great for stationery, because you can print a whole page picture at 10% or 20% of the original OPACITY, and it will show up like a ghost image or a background design. You can still write on top of it, and the words are easy to read because the picture is so faint.

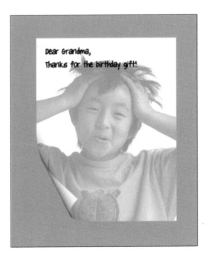

HINT!!

Have a lot of people to write to, and the same information to deliver? Type it in word-processing software and select a font that looks like handwriting for a personal look.

Easiest Envelope

After an awesome vacation, write a letter to a friend and tuck it in an envelope that looks like a postcard. The easiest way to make one is to start with a real envelope, and run it through the printer. But you can only do this if your printer can handle the thickness and small size of an envelope.

If your printer or word-processing software has an envelope TEMPLATE, you're home-free. Instead of typing in an address, INSERT a picture. In common software like Microsoft Word, select INSERT PHOTO. Then tug at the edges so it fills most of the space.

Make sure that pulling at the edge does not distort the image by stretching or scrunching it. Different software has different ways to enlarge the picture—some enlarge it proportionately, so it does not distort. If you find it distorting, you may have to check the instruction manual.

You'll need to know if your printer feeds the envelope in the long or short way. You may have to ROTATE the image, so it will look right when viewed normally (sideways or LANDSCAPE).

Without an envelope TEMPLATE, you'll need to be more creative.

Open a NEW document and pick a command called PAGE SETUP or DOCUMENT SETUP, or similar. Then click on your envelope size. Click LANDSCAPE mode if you want it to be right-side-up on the envelope. You may also have to select CUSTOM paper size in the printer menu if it doesn't list your exact envelope size.

Most printers will leave a small border on the edges of the envelope. Check and see if you printer MENU has a BORDERLESS option. If not, you can always use a magic marker to change this blank edge into a fancy decorative border.

Picture Hint

The final goal is to make an envelope that will still look good after you add stamps, and the "to" and "from" addresses. A photograph with a relatively simple area in the center for the address is important, so the post office can read the writing!

Use a black pen over light areas, and a silver or gold opaque metallic pen over dark areas. If all else fails, add a white sticker label.

Glossary

AUTOFLASH: The camera's automated flash mode. It usually fires the flash in low-light situations.

AUTOFOCUS: The camera automatically focuses on what it thinks is the main subject (on most cameras this is whatever is in the center of the frame).

BITMAP (BMP): A picture file format common on the Internet.

CLIPART: Digital drawings, animation, or photos that you can buy or get for free.

COMPOSITION: An art term for how a picture is designed.

COMPRESSION: A way of reducing the file size of a computer file (such as a digital picture). The JPEG picture format can be compressed to small sizes.

CONTRAST: A software tool that makes shadows darker and highlights brighter.

DELETE: Permanently erase a file or picture. When clearing all pictures from a memory card or memory stick it is sometimes called format or reformat.

DIGITAL ZOOM: A camera feature that makes your subject look closer. This is done electronically rather than with the lens. *See* optical zoom.

DIGITIZE: To turn a film image into a computer-friendly format.

DOCK: Some cameras have a special dish that you place your camera on to download photos to the computer (instead of a cord).

DOWNLOAD: To transfer pictures from your camera to computer, or Internet to computer. Also called upload.

DPI (DOTS PER INCH): A measurement that defines the number of dots in a print. Often used interchangeably with PPI.

DUOTONE: Basically a black-and-white photo that also has a secondary color.

DV (DIGITAL VIDEO): Movies that are saved in a computer file format rather than on videotape or film.

EQUIVALENT ISO: This figure indicates a camera's low-light capability, with a higher number being better. See page 27.

FILE SIZE: How much memory space a file (such as a digital picture) takes to store in a camera or computer's memory. High resolution pictures have a bigger file size than low resolution pictures.

FILL FLASH: A flash mode that fires the camera's built-in or accessory flash to add some front lighting to the subject.

FIREWIRE: A type of port to connect computers, cameras, scanners, etc., so they can transfer files between them.

FIXED-FOCUS: A camera that can't autofocus.

FOCUS LOCK: The autofocusing on most cameras is very center-oriented. focus lock enables you to take off-centered pictures that are properly focused.

FORMAT: *See* delete.

GIF: A picture file format common on the Internet. Common with clipart.

HIGH RESOLUTION: *See* resolution.

INSERT: A software command that adds a photo or type to a picture or document.

JPEG: A picture format that is a good choice for digital photos.

LOW RESOLUTION: *See* resolution.

MACRO: Close-up shooting capability.

MEGABYTE (MB): A measurement of file size. A high resolution photo may be over 2 MB.

MEGAPIXEL: 1,000,000 pixels. Often used to indicate the resolution of a camera.

MEMORY CARDS OR STICKS: Removable devices onto which your digital camera records pictures. They can be erased and reused over and over again. Cards with more MB can hold more pictures before they are full.

MP3: A file format for digital sound.

OPACITY: Software allows you to make an entire picture or a software tool (like stamp) solid (opaque) or see-through (transparent). 100% opacity is solid, while lower percentages become more transparent.

OPTICAL ZOOM: A camera feature that makes your subject look closer. This is done optically by zooming the lens from wide to tele. *See* digital zoom.

PANNING: A camera technique that helps you get sharper images, especially of moving subjects. See pages 56–57 for details.

PIXEL: A single picture element that, when combined with others, creates a digital photograph.

PLAYBACK: Reviewing pictures on the camera's monitor.

PLUG-AND-PLAY: A camera, scanner, or software that's so easy to use, you don't even need to read the instruction manual.

PORT: A place on your computer, camera, or scanner where you can connect it to another device. USB and firewire do this with cords. It can also be done with a wireless connection.

PPI (PIXELS PER INCH): A way to state a picture's resolution in terms of how densely the pixels are packed (for example, *there are 300 per inch,* or 300 ppi).

PRINTING TEMPLATE: A pre-designed page that helps you quickly print multiple photos on one sheet of paper.

RESOLUTION: An expression of how many pixels make up a digital image. More pixels (higher resolution) means more quality but larger file sizes. *See* dpi and ppi.

SCANNER: A machine that turns a print, film or flat artwork into a digital picture.

SCSI: An older, slower type of port to connect computers, cameras, scanners, etc., so they can transfer files between them.

SLR CAMERA: A single-lens reflex camera, often associated with professional photography. Most SLRs offer interchangeable lenses and advanced accessories.

TELE: A lens setting that makes the subject look closer than it actually is (not unlike binoculars).

TEMPLATE: *See* printing template.

TIFF: A picture file format used mostly by professionals.

TRANSPARENCY: *See* opacity.

UPLOAD: *See* download.

USB: A type of PORT to connect computers, cameras, scanners, etc., so they can transfer files between them.

VIEWFINDER: A viewing window that you bring up to your eye and look through to compose pictures.

WORLD WIDE WEB (WWW): A term that originally referred to the commercial sector of the Internet but is now synonymous with the Internet as a whole.

WIDE: A zoom lens setting that gives you a wider view of the scene (more included from right to left and top to bottom) than a TELE lens setting.

WIRELESS: A type of PORT to connect computers, cameras, scanners, etc., so they can transfer files between them. Unlike USB or firewire, it does not require any cords.

ZOOM: A type of lens that allows you to zoom from a WIDE view of the scene to a closer look at your subject (tele).

Metric Conversion Chart

½ inch = 1.3 cm
1 inch = 2.5 cm
2 inches = 5.1 cm
3 inches = 7.6 cm
4 inches = 10.2 cm
5 inches = 12.7 cm
8½ inches = 21.6 cm
11 inches = 27.9 cm

Index